INTRODUCTION

Just when everything lines up in life exactly as we want it, we experience an unanticipated disaster that spoils everything. Our health declines, someone dies, a spouse leaves, bills pile up, friends reject us, our child makes a bad decision.…

Such setbacks can sometimes be overwhelming. We can lose hope that life will ever get better. But wait. We are literally wasting our lives if we live with this kind of despair. If we always complain about how bad life is or how hopeless the situation seems, we're going to be miserable. Such an attitude keeps us from moving forward in our lives. Instead, when setbacks show up, call on Jesus. He offers hope. He reaches out to lift us up when our world feels like it's falling apart. So when things go wrong in your life, stop searching for an escape route and instead invite the problem in, knowing that Jesus is less than a heartbeat away. He's coaching us to use our inner strength, perseverance, and determination to bounce back and get on our feet again, stronger and better.

I'm glad you picked up this book. I wrote it with you in mind. Take your time with it. Walk slowly, every day, through each reflection. The "Simple to do" suggestions following each reflection will help you take positive steps toward change, and the "Follow it through" prayers will help you renew your commitment to Jesus. Above all, welcome Jesus into your life during these weeks of Lent, and let him be the anchor of your soul.

TWENTY-THIRD PUBLICATIONS A division of Bayard, Inc | Bayard CEO: Hugues de Foucauld
One Montauk Avenue, Suite 200; New London, CT 06320 | (860) 437-3012 or (800) 321-0411
www.twentythirdpublications.com

Copyright ©2022 Joseph F. Sica. All rights reserved. No part of this publication may be reproduced in any manner without prior written permission of the publisher. Write to the Permissions Editor.

ISBN: 978-1-62785-667-6 | Cover image: ©Shutterstock.com / Pavel Klasek | Printed in the U.S.A.

MARCH 2 — Ash Wednesday
JOEL 2:12–18 • 2 CORINTHIANS 5:20—6:2 • MATTHEW 6:1–6, 16–18

We're All Banged Up

"And your Father, who sees what is hidden, will repay you."
» MATTHEW 6:18

I was watching the movie *Seabiscuit* when the actor's words slammed into my soul: "You don't throw a whole life away just because it's banged up a little."

We are all "banged up a little." We have scars, wounds, and broken places. We also have new challenges. Someone we work with may be difficult to talk to, a significant other may have moved on, there may be a misunderstanding or sudden change in a delicate relationship, a routine checkup may reveal a serious problem....

Even though we are bruised by these events, we are blessed to be able to pick up the pieces and recover with greater clarity and determination. In every circumstance, God gives us a warehouse of treasures to help us bounce back. Lent is the perfect season to uncover those treasures, find strength, and change direction. We only need to explore these lessons, give of ourselves, and pray to discover the wealth of treasures inside. Open yourself up to new ideas, and let go of old habits and behaviors!

SIMPLE TO DO ▸ Choose one habit or behavior that you want to change. Turn it over to Jesus and ask him to help you kick the habit or stop the behavior.

FOLLOW IT THROUGH ▸ *Jesus, with you all things are possible. Help me to anchor myself to you and believe that you will heal my broken places. Amen.*

MARCH 3 ■ Thursday after Ash Wednesday ■ *Saint Katharine Drexel*

DEUTERONOMY 30:15–20 • LUKE 9:22–25

This Is Who I Am!

"What profit is there for one to gain the whole world yet lose or forfeit himself?" » LUKE 9:25

Imagine a life where we can let the world see us—and we can see ourselves—as we truly are: vulnerable, valuable, hurting, hoping, dreaming, believing, yearning for love and acceptance. To do this, we need to develop a sense of worth and a capacity for positive self-regard that comes deep from inside ourselves. To sustain this, we must avoid those who drag us down and be present to those people who build us up.

Negative people criticize and compare us. It may come as a direct hit ("you're stupid") or be more subtle ("your sister always makes me proud"). When we're attacked like this, we start thinking "I'm not good enough" and "I can't." Positive people encourage us to be real and genuine. They remind us of our strengths, recognize our greatness, and encourage us to strive for what is best for us.

As you begin this lenten season, claim your power. Say: "This is who I am. If you cannot accept me, leave me alone and move on."

SIMPLE TO DO ▶ Get clear about what you want to do and make it a priority. Write out the script of your life. Then, take at least one action step each day this Lent to make it happen.

FOLLOW IT THROUGH ▶ *Jesus, my friend, help me to be my own person and to stand up for myself. Help me resist those who drag me down. Amen.*

MARCH 4 ■ Friday after Ash Wednesday ■ *Saint Casimir*

ISAIAH 58:1–9A • MATTHEW 9:14–15

Laughter Heals

"Can the wedding guests mourn as long as the bridegroom is with them?" » MATTHEW 9:15

I was invited to speak at a program for cancer survivors and their families called "Hysterical living for the humor-impaired." After my talk, a woman shared that her doctors were amazed at how well she was doing. They had been skeptical about her chances for survival, but she was planning for an active and vibrant future. Her secret? Laughter therapy! In addition to her good medical care, she attributed her recovery to her sense of humor and her ability to find the lighter side of things, even on the toughest days.

Laughter as therapy can be experienced by anyone. Some of the happiest people I know seem to have no particular reason to be joyful. It's all about attitude and expectation.

Soul-saving laughter that springs freely from our very core can help us reduce stress, elevate mood, boost our immune system, and foster instant relaxation. This Lent, we have every reason to rejoice. The "bridegroom" is still with us.

SIMPLE TO DO ▶ Arrange a joke-exchange evening with family and friends. Or rent a humorous movie and watch it alone or with others. Start a humor collection of cartoons, books, and anything else that helps you laugh.

FOLLOW IT THROUGH ▶ *Jesus, my friend, help me find laughter during life's tense moments. Amen.*

MARCH 5 — Saturday after Ash Wednesday

ISAIAH 58:9B–14 • LUKE 5:27–32

We Are All Cheerleaders

And he said to him, "Follow me." » LUKE 5:27

Have you ever said something and then immediately wished you hadn't? If so, you know the power of thoughtless words. They can crush, demean, and intimidate in seconds. Disparaging remarks, accusations, and complaints get attention but often at a price.

Positive words, on the other hand, can affirm, encourage, and motivate. People who have good relationships know the power of their words. They realize that those around them can never receive too much encouragement.

People around us are starving for encouragement. If we want good relationships, we need to learn how to be a genuine encourager. It doesn't take much to encourage someone. It can be a short note that says, "I prayed for you today" or a card in the mail or voice message that says, "I was thinking of you." It only takes a minute, and it has a ripple effect, helping the person to feel appreciated and valued.

SIMPLE TO DO ▸ Write genuine notes of encouragement to your family or friends. Share special quotes, poems, or verses. The best thing about notes is that there is no cost involved. You can leave them on pillows, bulletin boards, in lunch boxes, or on car windows. Gentle encouragement builds confidence and is much appreciated.

FOLLOW IT THROUGH ▸ *Jesus, my friend, when life is overwhelming, help me remember to lighten someone else's day with an encouraging word. Amen.*

MARCH 6 ■ First Sunday of Lent

DEUTERONOMY 26:4–10 • ROMANS 10:8–13 • LUKE 4:1–13

It's Time to Wake Up!

When the devil had finished all the tempting, he left him, to await another opportunity. » LUKE 4:13

On their twentieth wedding anniversary, Jack was stunned to learn that his wife wanted a divorce. He told me, "I was suddenly jolted out of a secure reality, confronted with circumstances, issues, and challenges that I hoped I would never have to face."

Wake-up calls shock and surprise us. One moment we're going about our business, and the next moment, everything has changed.

We can learn a lot from these wake-up calls. They may be painful and frightening, but after we get through the initial trauma, we can often find opportunities to grow and improve.

Losses, illnesses, accidents, and tragedies are never expected. When they show up, we can welcome them and discover the message they give us. They can motivate us to analyze our values, define what's precious, realign our priorities, and focus on what needs our attention. No matter how difficult a wake-up call is to accept, consider it a gift to be unwrapped and embraced with enthusiasm and gratitude.

SIMPLE TO DO ▶ During troublesome times, write down your wake-up calls in a journal. What truths are they telling you about yourself? How are they renewing and reviving your spirit?

FOLLOW IT THROUGH ▶ *Jesus, my friend, help me be aware and alert to all that's happening in my life so I can grow from each experience. Amen.*

MARCH 7 ▪ Monday of the First Week ▪ *Saints Perpetua and Felicity*

LEVITICUS 19:1–2, 11–18 • MATTHEW 25:31–46

Little Acts of Kindness

"Whatever you did for one of these brothers and sisters of mine, you did for me." » MATTHEW 25:40

One of the most memorable Christmas cards I ever received was from my dear friend, Mary Lou. It was a single piece of heavy white paper with the word "others" written diagonally across the card in red ink.

Isn't that what Christianity is all about? Others? From time to time, it's good to measure how much we affect others and touch their lives.

How do we relate to others—our family, friends, neighbors, strangers, and yes, even our enemies? Many of us would like to have a big impact on other people's lives. But we must never take for granted the importance of the little things we do: a pat on the back, a kiss on the cheek, a nod of the head. These actions have the power to heal wounds, build bridges, and encourage and comfort others.

Doing little things for others is contagious too. Our goodness toward one person will often prompt that person to do something good for someone else.

SIMPLE TO DO ▶ Recall someone who has had a significant impact on your life and contact him or her this week. Share how much his or her actions mean to you.

FOLLOW IT THROUGH ▶ *Jesus, my friend, it's often the little acts of kindness that bring growth and gladness to others. Help me share many such acts this Lent. Amen.*

MARCH 8 ■ Tuesday of the First Week ■ *Saint John of God*

ISAIAH 55:10–11 • MATTHEW 6:7–15

Forgive and Move On!

"Forgive us our debts, as we forgive our debtors."
» MATTHEW 6:12

Betsy was devastated when her husband left her. She was angry, resentful, and bitter.

I suggested to Betsy that she forgive her husband for his actions and forgive herself for any part she may have played in their break-up. She was stunned: "Forgive him! Are you crazy? I'd die first! I want him to hurt like I hurt!" She was consumed with revenge. She kept reliving the hurt and telling the story over and over again.

Betsy's behavior is typical of many of us. When we're overwhelmed with rage, it's a challenge to realize our value, regain our power, let go of the pain, and then move on. Forgiveness is not about approving the hurtful behavior of another. It's about giving up the rage and resentment that we feel entitled to and offering acceptance of and detachment from the situation and the person involved.

Resentment and revenge are heavy loads to carry. If we hope to be forgiven for our own shortcomings, we might start by forgiving others for theirs.

SIMPLE TO DO ▶ Plan a "two thumbs-up" night with your family and friends. Select a movie with a forgiveness theme. Watch it and share the challenges of forgiveness.

FOLLOW IT THROUGH ▶ *Jesus, my friend, help me forgive, release resentment, and get on with my life. Amen.*

MARCH 9 ■ Wednesday of the First Week ■ *Saint Frances of Rome*

JONAH 3:1–10 • LUKE 11:29–32

Golden or Lost Opportunities?

"No sign will be given except the sign of Jonah. You have a greater one than Jonah here." » LUKE 11:29, 32

Wendy looked at me with sadness in her eyes. "Is death always followed by feelings of missed opportunities?" she asked. She had had no idea that her father knew he was dying, or that her visit with him during Christmas would be her last. She hadn't known that he had treasured every moment and wanted her to stay a while longer. She only knew that she had a plane to catch. Now she regrets missing out on those final precious moments with her dad.

How often do we wish for a second chance? Each day we are given opportunities but often miss them because we're preoccupied with other things.

Be alert for these golden opportunities! Pray to notice a hidden tear, a tone of voice, or a look of loneliness or despair. Look for the pain and extend compassion. Be sensitive to what is needed. Sometimes, just our presence is enough. The real tragedy is to reach the end of our lives and realize that we missed an opportunity to have made someone's life just a little bit better.

SIMPLE TO DO ▶ Be deliberate about spending time with the people you love. Remember to listen, to hug, and to say "I love you" while you still have the chance.

FOLLOW IT THROUGH ▶ *Jesus, my friend, open my eyes a little wider to see that every moment is filled with golden opportunities just waiting to be embraced. Amen.*

MARCH 10 ▪ Thursday of the First Week

ESTHER C:12, 14–16, 23–25 • MATTHEW 7:7–12

What Goes Around Comes Around

"Do to others whatever you would have them do to you."
» MATTHEW 7:12

Relationships are rarely simple. The people we love can cause us the greatest pain, and our closest friends may be the ones who disappoint us the most. And who among us has not experienced the puzzle of a relationship that flourishes with affection and then fades without warning?

Many relationships end because we're overconfident, not prepared, or unrealistic in our expectations. Others wither because we do not invest the upkeep, time, or care that they require. But if we cannot live in total harmony with one another, can we at least offer our respect? Can we not find a way to coexist peacefully?

The process of relating to others can be compared to a boomerang. Our thoughts, words, and actions return to us sooner or later with astonishing accuracy. Jesus gives us a boomerang that soars up and away and curves back into our lives with precision. It's called the Golden Rule: "I want to be treated the way I treat others." Start right where you are. Whatever you throw out—anger, resentment, compassion, or forgiveness—will eventually bounce back into your life.

SIMPLE TO DO ▶ Write down all the reasons you love each person in your life. Then, when the going gets tough, find that list and read it.

FOLLOW IT THROUGH ▶ *Jesus, my friend, you've taught me that I always have a choice. It is up to me to choose how I treat others and how I want to be treated. Amen.*

MARCH 11 ■ Friday of the First Week

EZEKIEL 18:21–28 • MATTHEW 5:20–26

Refocus and Forgive

"Go first and be reconciled and then come and offer your gift."
» MATTHEW 5:24

Most of us have one thing in common: at one time or another, we've been hurt by someone we love. In my ministry, I've seen hundreds of people who continue to harbor past hurts. They stay tied up in knots because they refuse to forgive. It may be difficult to forgive, but when we continue to suffer from these hurtful feelings, we give our power away. We have to work to change these feelings. It's a journey, and it's a decision. If we continue to hold on to our grudges, we are only damaging ourselves. It is quite likely that the person who hurt us has moved on. Can we move on too? Can we decide to feel differently?

Forgiving is not about approving the hurtful behavior. It's about healing the memory so that it no longer rules our lives. We can do that by redirecting our focus and our energy and doing something for ourselves every day that helps us to feel better about our lives.

SIMPLE TO DO ▶ Forgiving those who have hurt us is not a one-shot deal. It is a journey, and it begins with a choice. God gives us a certain amount of energy to spend each day, and only we can decide how to use it. Spend your energy this Lent by offering forgiveness and letting go of the hurt.

FOLLOW IT THROUGH ▶ *Jesus, my friend, help me make peace with "what is" and then allow forgiveness to rule my heart. Amen.*

MARCH 12 ■ Saturday of the First Week

DEUTERONOMY 26:16–19 • MATTHEW 5:43–48

How Can I Love You?

"Love your enemies and pray for those who persecute you."
» MATTHEW 5:44

How do we deal with the difficult people in our lives? We don't have to turn away from them or let them affect us. Jesus shows us another way: we can love them! When we analyze the word love, letter by letter, we discover that it's a powerful, four-step force that can help us disarm difficult people.

Learn that difficult people relate from the negative side of everything. They often are unaware of their hurtful behavior and have no interest in how they affect us.

Overcome the desire to fight back or beat difficult people at their own game. Simply do not respond to their negative comments.

Vow to openly express your feelings. If someone is very negative with you, simply say, "This is who I am, this is how I feel, and I do not appreciate your negative comments."

Encourage yourself not to give up. See yourself as the powerful person you are.

Difficult people seem to take away our power when we least expect it. Only the power of love can render them powerless.

SIMPLE TO DO ▸ Practice the power of love with difficult people today. Write out the words above, memorize them, use them often, and teach them to others.

FOLLOW IT THROUGH ▸ *Jesus, my friend, it's easy for me to love likable people. But people who get on my nerves are challenging. Starting today, help me look only at their good qualities and love them. Amen.*

MARCH 13 — Second Sunday of Lent

GENESIS 15:5–12, 17–18 • PHILIPPIANS 3:17—4:1 *or* 3:20—4:1 • LUKE 9:28B–36

Caught Up in Glory

While he was praying, the appearance of his face changed and his clothes became dazzling white. » LUKE 9:29

At one time or another, we will all have the experience of losing someone we love. We do not "get over" grief. We manage it by grieving in different ways and at different stages. For some of us, it takes months or years to get through it, and even many years later a tender memory can suddenly bring up a flood of tears. We need to honor our feelings and allow ourselves the time we need to heal.

Months after my mother's death, there were times when I thought: "I need to tell this to Mom." Then I remembered that she was gone, and a new wave of grief swept over me. In the stillness of my heart, I was comforted by one simple word: "Someday."

Most of us will eventually arrive at acceptance and hope, and as we see in today's gospel, God surrounds our "beloved ones" with glorious light.

SIMPLE TO DO ▶ Decide to be a friend to someone you know who is grieving. Be patient. Listen. Let the person know that he or she is not alone.

FOLLOW IT THROUGH ▶ *Jesus, my friend, you were enveloped in God's wonderful light. May my loved ones be caught up in the light of God's glory. Amen.*

MARCH 14 ■ Monday of the Second Week

DANIEL 9:4B–10 • LUKE 6:36–38

Walk in Their Shoes

"Stop judging and you will not be judged."
» LUKE 6:37

Agnes tends to make judgments about people quickly, especially when they're not acting the way she thinks they should. She's not the only one who judges. We all do. We analyze the people around us, those we live with, the leaders in our community, and even total strangers. We scrutinize the way they walk, their clothing, hairstyle, skin color, ethnic background, occupation, and everything else. We make judgments so easily that often we're not even aware that we're judging. When we "sum up" another person, it prevents us from seeing the goodness that lies below the surface and beyond their appearance.

A non-judgmental attitude, however, causes understanding, compassion, and acceptance to flow into a person's life and helps them grow. We can choose to become the person we were tempted to judge, to step into their circumstance for a while, and to see life differently through their eyes. This view may change our attitude completely.

SIMPLE TO DO ▶ Think back to your favorite professor or teacher. How did he or she treat students? Did he or she give them the benefit of the doubt? Praise more and criticize less? Try to remember a story from his or her life that illustrates these ideals. And then model it!

FOLLOW IT THROUGH ▶ *Jesus, my friend, you could not have been clearer: stop judging. Help me detach and allow. Amen.*

MARCH 15 — Tuesday of the Second Week

ISAIAH 1:10, 16–20 • MATTHEW 23:1–12

The Power to Influence

"Therefore, do and observe all things, but do not follow their example." » MATTHEW 23:3

Each one of us carries the flu—not the disease kind—but the in-"flu"-ential kind. Every person we encounter will be affected by us. We can be a positive and important influence on others by doing what is good and what is right. If we intentionally direct our influence, we can be incredibly powerful. All it takes is two simple steps.

1. **Smile.** When we smile, people light up and smile back. There is just something about the smallest kind word, or the simplest smile, that can make a difference and turn someone's whole day around.
2. **Support.** Reach into the pain of life where people are broken, hurting, or hopeless. Give them emotional encouragement, care, and support. Tell them, "I care about you. I care about what you are going through." This support will leave a lasting impact on their lives.

SIMPLE TO DO ▶ Draw a circle on a piece of paper and write the words: "My sphere of influence." Then write down the names of all the people you could influence in a positive and powerful way. Under each name, be specific: how could you positively affect their lives? Then take that action, smile, offer your support, and, of course, include them in your prayers during Lent.

FOLLOW IT THROUGH ▶ *Jesus, help me be more intentional by smiling and supporting those who feel alone, afraid, and injured. Amen.*

MARCH 16 ■ Wednesday of the Second Week

JEREMIAH 18:18–20 • MATTHEW 20:17–28

Accepting "What Is"

Then the mother of the sons of Zebedee approached him with her sons, wishing to ask him to do something. » MATTHEW 20:20

I love the cartoon of the infant lying in a bassinet with a scowl on his face. The caption reads: World's Youngest Recorded Snit. "Snit" is one of my favorite words because it describes perfectly a typical response to disappointment.

Disappointment results from the unexpected. Life does not always turn out the way we planned. When these detours happen, our challenge is to accept the current situation and not spend a lot of time wishing for what could have been.

When we embrace life, we accept all of it, even the surprises. Wanting things to be different or to go away is not life-affirming. Managing disappointment is summed up in the Serenity Prayer:

God, grant me the serenity to accept the things I cannot change, the courage to change the things I can, and the wisdom to know the difference.

This is true acceptance.

SIMPLE TO DO ▶ One of the best cures for disappointment is to serve others. Doing something nice could be serving a meal, caring for kids, cleaning a home, doing laundry, or offering a ride to the grocery store. These are all ways that we could feel better about our situation and help someone else feel better too.

FOLLOW IT THROUGH ▶ *Jesus, my friend, the next time I'm disappointed, I'm going to "roll with the punches" and look for windows of opportunity to grow and help others. Amen.*

MARCH 17 ◼ Thursday of the Second Week ◼ *Saint Patrick*

JEREMIAH 17:5–10 • LUKE 16:19–31

Share Your Heart

"You received what was good during your lifetime while Lazarus received what was bad." » LUKE 16:25

My friend Gene was dying. Harriet, his love of two years, had proposed marriage. At their wedding, I was proud to pronounce them husband and wife. As they left the church, Gene turned to Harriet and said, "Sweetheart, this is the happiest day of my life."

Ten days later, Gene died. Harriet had the memory of their great love and joyful wedding to keep her strong. Although brokenhearted, she never once complained of bitterness or regret. Instead, she was able to convert her sorrow into a service of healing for others. With her gentle, steady presence, she now helps other men and women who are grieving the loss of their loved one. She is never too busy to volunteer at hospice, take a phone call late at night, or sit with someone who is grieving. Harriet reminds us that even when we feel powerless, we can always offer a kind heart.

SIMPLE TO DO ▸ There are many ways we can help each other. We can write a note, prepare a meal, give a hug, send flowers, or sit quietly and listen to what needs to be said. Sometimes our greatest sorrow in life can be the catalyst we need for discovering our unique gift to the world.

FOLLOW IT THROUGH ▸ *Jesus, my friend, I can change sorrow into service by noticing people who are hurting and by doing something to ease their pain. Help me recognize these opportunities for healing. Amen.*

MARCH 18 ■ Friday of the Second Week ■ *Saint Cyril of Jerusalem*

GENESIS 37:3–4, 12–13A, 17B–28A • MATTHEW 21:33–43, 45–46

Being Hurt by Those We Love

*"Finally he sent his son to them thinking,
'They will respect my son.'"* » MATTHEW 21:37

Some of the hardest blows in life come from the people we love. The deeper we love, the greater we hurt.

When we are deeply hurt, our first reaction may be to get even. Deep down, we know that hurting another will never resolve anything. We must refuse to participate in this kind of behavior and refrain from actions that could fuel the fire.

Sometimes a hurtful word from someone we love is not meant as an attack. Instead, it could be a cry for help or an effort to get our attention. Listen closely. Ask with genuine concern: "What is the real problem?" Make it safe for the person to openly express his or her feelings. Ask what could bring you closer together. Because we love them, we can work harder to resolve the problem and restore the relationship.

SIMPLE TO DO ▸ Reflect on these questions and write the answers in a journal: Should I allow someone who hurts me to stay in my life, or should I shut them out to protect myself from further hurt? Is there something I can say or do to make amends or resolve the situation?

FOLLOW IT THROUGH ▸ *Jesus, my friend, when you were hurt again and again by those you loved, you continued to love them and seek the best for them. Help me model your example. Amen.*

MARCH 19 ■ Saint Joseph

2 SAMUEL 7:4–5A, 12–14A, 16 • ROMANS 4:13, 16–18, 22 • MATTHEW 1:16, 18–21, 24A *or* LUKE 2:41–51A

Face the Unexpected with Faith

"Joseph, son of David, do not be afraid to take Mary your wife into your home." » MATTHEW 1:20

Everything was going fine for Mary and Joseph—they were in love. They looked forward to getting married and raising a family. Surprise! God had a different plan.

Life's surprises will always catch us off guard. The only way to turn is toward *faith* and *faces*:

Faith: When we're hit with the unexpected, we must believe God is big enough to take care of us. We must ask God to give us what we need. God won't disappoint us.

Faces: We don't have the strength to survive alone. We need faces that are touchable, approachable, available. We want a place to cry, a person to care, the security of friends who will share our hurt. Shared joy is double joy. Shared sorrow is half a sorrow.

It's easy to collapse when we're hit with the unexpected. Yet if we do, we might find ourselves near the end of our lives thinking: "If I'd had more faith in God, what might I have done? If I'd reached out further, what might I have become?"

SIMPLE TO DO ▶ Give up a favorite activity and use the time to talk with a friend or neighbor who could use some propping up.

FOLLOW IT THROUGH ▶ *Jesus, you have given me two hands—one for receiving help and the other for giving help. Show me the way to use both my hands. Amen.*

MARCH 20 — Third Sunday of Lent

EXODUS 3:1–8A, 13–15 • 1 CORINTHIANS 10:1–6, 10–12 • LUKE 13:1–9 *or*, **FOR YEAR A:** EXODUS 17:3–7 • ROMANS 5:1–2, 5–8 • JOHN 4:5–42 *or* 4:5–15, 19B–26, 39A, 40–42

Patience Is a Virtue

"Sir, leave it for this year, and I shall cultivate the ground around it." » LUKE 13:8

Nature offers an infinite variety of plants that delight us. It would be silly to demand that they reveal a new bud or leaf when we think it's time. They will grow and flower at their own pace.

Patience is not a highly cultivated virtue in our society. How we deal with the interruptions, inconveniences, and irritations of life is a test of patience. We want to have the answers, now. We want to change our lives, now. We want fame and fortune, now. We overlook the fact that these things take careful analysis, thoughtful consideration, and quiet deliberation. This is especially true of our relationships. We want the perfect person and the ideal relationship. If this does not happen quickly, we bail out early and disregard the time, endurance, and steadiness needed to build a great relationship. Practicing patience implies that we are willing to bear suffering, endure delays, and persevere when things become slow or difficult.

SIMPLE TO DO ▸ In your journal, write a short poem, song, or paragraph about each of the following sayings that promote patience: Let go and let God. Easy does it. One day at a time. Today is the first day of the rest of my life. First things first.

FOLLOW IT THROUGH ▸ *Jesus, my friend, thank you for being patient with me. Help me be patient with people in my life who are struggling. Amen.*

MARCH 21 ■ Monday of the Third Week

2 KINGS 5:1–15AB • LUKE 4:24–30

Hooked on Pleasing

He passed through the midst of them and went away.
» LUKE 4:30

After fifteen years of marriage, Elaine had allowed a disturbing pattern to develop. When she wasn't working full-time, she took care of the chores and the kids. Her husband, on the other hand, spent most of his free time playing golf. Elaine felt dumped on and isolated but said nothing. But her feelings were taking their toll.

People-pleasers go overboard to make other people happy. They constantly struggle to draw the line between their own needs and the demands of others. They do not realize that always putting someone else first causes serious consequences. Elaine always said yes when she really wanted to say no.

Many of us shy away from conflict just to keep the peace. But there is a huge reward for staying true to ourselves and not allowing the attitudes, judgments, and opinions of others to rule us. For the first time, we can experience wholeness. When we speak our mind, demand respect, and expect to be treated fairly, we will honor the magnificent person we are and stand in our glory.

SIMPLE TO DO ▸ Identify those people in your life you are most tempted to please at the expense of your own self-care. How might you deal with them differently?

FOLLOW IT THROUGH ▸ *Jesus, my friend, by trying to please everyone else, I am sacrificing my own integrity. Give me the courage to speak my deepest thoughts and express what I am truly feeling. Amen.*

MARCH 22 ■ Tuesday of the Third Week

DANIEL 3:25, 34–43 • MATTHEW 18:21–35

Call Me If You Need Me

"Should you not have shown compassion to your fellow servant?" » MATTHEW 18:33

I love Winnie the Pooh. In one episode, Pooh Bear walks along the riverbank, sees his donkey friend floating downstream, and asks if he's fallen in. The anguished donkey answers: "Silly of me, wasn't it?" Pooh ignores his friend's pleading eyes and remarks that he should have been more careful. Almost with a yawn, Pooh Bear says, "I think you're sinking." With that, the drowning donkey asks Pooh if he would mind rescuing him. So Pooh pulls him out. The donkey apologizes for being such a bother, and Pooh, still unconcerned yet ever so courteous, responds, "Don't be silly, you should have said something sooner."

This episode reflects the world of real people in real need. How many of our friends are soaked to the ears and about to drown? Maybe it is a struggle at work, a nagging physical burden, financial worries, a relationship problem, or grief pulling them down. Yet we keep our distance. True compassion, however, produces concern and action. Compassionate people feel the struggles of another by reaching out to them in their suffering.

SIMPLE TO DO ▶ Compassion means taking the time to really listen. Resolve today to truly listen to someone until you understand what he or she is feeling.

FOLLOW IT THROUGH ▶ *Jesus, my friend, help me take my eyes off myself so I can see what is going on in the lives of those around me. Amen.*

MARCH 23 ■ Wednesday of the Third Week ■ *Saint Turibius of Mogrovejo*

DEUTERONOMY 4:1, 5–9 • MATTHEW 5:17–19

Giving Our Best

"Whoever breaks these commandments and teaches others to do so will be called least in the kingdom." » MATTHEW 5:19

A lady wrote to advice columnist Ann Landers: "My husband doesn't talk to me any more. He just sits there night after night, reading the newspaper or watching television. When I ask him a question, he grunts 'uh-huh.' Sometimes he doesn't even respond. There are times when I wonder why we ever got married."

When we first fall in love, we look for ways to show how much we care. But after the newness begins to fade, sometimes we take our partner for granted. Our best moments are saved for work or for friends. We come home exhausted, stressed out, and irritated.

A good relationship models any successful business venture. It requires team effort, appreciation, productivity, understanding, and compassion. It requires the assignment and sharing of work responsibilities, and the best part is, it has the added benefits of love, support, and intimacy to enjoy.

SIMPLE TO DO ▶ Try a little kindness. Talk to your partner. Reveal what is bothering you and request his or her feedback. Plan to do relaxing things together. Make a point to be caring. Ask for and give understanding. Do something special because you genuinely want to, and watch the relationship deepen.

FOLLOW IT THROUGH ▶ *Jesus, my friend, it is time for me to put down the newspaper, turn off the television, and look in the eyes of the person I love. Amen.*

MARCH 24 ■ Thursday of the Third Week

JEREMIAH 7:23–28 • LUKE 11:14–23

Lower the Temperature!

"Every kingdom divided against itself is laid waste. Any house torn by dissension falls." » LUKE 11:17

Dolores and Philip were trying to find a parking place. As Dolores attempted to squeeze the car into one place and then another, her husband started yelling, "You can't park there!" The louder he got, the angrier she became. By the time they finally parked, they were practically enemies—all because of a parking place.

Conflict is a fact of life. Personalities clash and feelings get hurt. It's not bad that we sometimes rub each other the wrong way—that's only human. What is unfortunate is the way we handle these situations. Some people yell and scream when issues surface; others cry, blame, hit below the belt, and use derogatory remarks.

Yet it is gentleness that leads to reconciliation. When there is a need to address a problem, follow this plan: Affirm the positive. Confess your own responsibility—honestly and specifically. Explain, rather than attack. Wait for your anger to cool. Refrain from words like "always" and "never." Keep focused on the main issue and work toward resolution, not blame.

SIMPLE TO DO ▶ Resolving conflict is not the most pleasant task, but create the time for it today. Get inside the other person's world and search to understand.

FOLLOW IT THROUGH ▶ *Jesus, my friend, help me examine the situations that keep me churning. Rather than being resentful, help me look at my responsibility and work for positive change. Amen.*

MARCH 25 ▪ The Annunciation of the Lord

ISAIAH 7:10–14; 8:10 • HEBREWS 10:4–10 • LUKE 1:26–38

Face Life Fearlessly

"Do not be afraid, Mary, for you have found favor with God."
» LUKE 1:30

With heart pounding, Mary worried about having a baby. Although panic raced through her mind, the angel calmed her and eliminated doubts about her pregnancy, allowing her to overcome her fears.

We can't let our lives be ruled by fear or we'll enjoy very few experiences.

So it's time to face your fears and forget about them; time to change your "What if…?" thinking into "I can handle this with God's guidance!" thinking.

Look fear in the eye and ask yourself two questions: "What's the worst thing that can happen?" and "How will I deal with it?" Write down positive steps you can take to face your fears. Be realistic, but believe that, with God's help, you have the strength to handle anything.

Then let it go and move ahead. Repeat these practices, and you'll find your self-confidence rising to high levels.

SIMPLE TO DO ▶ On a "Fear Management Scale," where would you rate yourself? Are you a 1—"I'm often paralyzed by fear"? or a 10—"I almost never let fear stop me"? What would you like your score to be? Listen to God's most repeated command in Scripture: Fear not. That sentence is repeated 366 times in the Bible. There must be a reason!

FOLLOW IT THROUGH ▶ *Jesus, with you, I can handle any fear. Amen.*

MARCH 26 ■ Saturday of the Third Week

HOSEA 6:1–6 • LUKE 18:9–14

The Power to Change

"O God, be merciful to me a sinner." » LUKE 18:13

We believe that we have the power to change. Without this belief, New Year's resolutions and recovery programs would be useless. Without this hope, broken relationships would never mend and churches would have no reason to exist.

Still, we seem to fear change and resist it. We hear all the time that some people will never change. But change is always possible.

Change begins with a yearning for something more authentic. We reach a point when we say, "I've had enough," and we ask, "Is there something better?" Only then are we alive to the possibility of becoming someone new in each moment.

We must resolve to give up our resistance and dance a new step. When we do, we will surely discover that change is our greatest source of happiness and continued growth.

SIMPLE TO DO ▶ How do you want to change? Get clear about what you want. Write it down. Visualize it. Act as if it's already happened. What does it feel like? Breathe it, see it, and know it, every day. Combine this vision with gratitude for the abundance you already have in your life.

FOLLOW IT THROUGH ▶ *Jesus, my friend, it takes a lot of courage to release the familiar and embrace the new. In change, there is growth. Help me grow into the powerful, joyous being I am meant to be. Amen.*

MARCH 27 ▪ Fourth Sunday of Lent

JOSHUA 5:9A, 10–12 • 2 CORINTHIANS 5:17–21 • LUKE 15:1–3, 11–32 *or,*
FOR YEAR A: 1 SAMUEL 16:1B, 6–7, 10–13A • EPHESIANS 5:8–14 • JOHN 9:1–41 *or* 9:1, 6–9, 13–17, 34–38

Keeping Memories Alive

"How many hired hands at my father's place have more than enough to eat, while here I am starving!" » LUKE 15:17

Memories may bubble up when we least expect it and fill our hearts with laughter and delight. It could be a faint aroma, a whiff of perfume, the fragrance of flowers, or the musty smell of a closet that cause our childhood memories to surface.

The prodigal son relied on his memories for survival. He was tired, alone, hungry, and out of money. His intuition invited and inspired him to swallow his pride and remember the kind things his father had done for him. He was guided to return home and reestablish his relationship with his dad, who loved him so much.

We can reestablish our own relationships by keeping our good memories alive. Such memories can lift our spirit and give us the courage to cope with the nitty-gritty of life. They help us not only honor our deeply held values but also consciously define who we are in each moment.

SIMPLE TO DO ▸ Save some of your precious memories this Lent by scrapbooking. Tackle the project with your family. You will talk, laugh, and even cry together as each photo or memento reminds you of a shared experience.

FOLLOW IT THROUGH ▸ *Jesus, my friend, I cherish the healing and humorous memories that I carry within my heart. Amen.*

MARCH 28 ■ Monday of the Fourth Week

ISAIAH 65:17–21 • JOHN 4:43–54

Embrace the Unknown

The man believed what Jesus said to him and left.
» JOHN 4:50

If we knew what each day would bring, there would be no need for free will or faith. What we do with what we are given is how we create meaning in our lives. It's a waste of our precious time to dread the future. It's much better that we use our energy to be here now and live our lives with generosity and grace.

When we stop dreading each day's stresses and surprises and meet them with a sense of humor, we're not rattled when our day doesn't go as planned. As New Yorker cartoonist Gahan Wilson once remarked: "Life essentially doesn't work. So it's the basis of endless humor."

We are alive. This moment is all we have! Love deeply, work hard, and play hard! Don't waste precious time with worry! Stop struggling, make peace with what is, and commit to doing your best. This doesn't mean bad things won't happen, but your response to them is a choice, and misery is optional.

SIMPLE TO DO ▶ On an index card, write the words: "Let my light shine." Wrap it around a candle and give it to someone who needs to clear away apathy, doubt, and fear. Then help this person light the candle and let it shine.

FOLLOW IT THROUGH ▶ *Jesus, my friend, help me say yes to life and live with generosity, humor, and grace. Let my life shine, especially during difficult times. Amen.*

MARCH 29 ■ Tuesday of the Fourth Week

EZEKIEL 47:1–9, 12 • JOHN 5:1–16

Listen from the Heart

"I have no one to put me in the pool when the water is stirred up." » JOHN 5:7

When someone is facing a crisis and is tied up in knots, they long for someone who will be there for them. Some days they'll want to talk. Other days, they'll want us to sit with them in silence. Other times, they'll want us to just hold them as they cry. The only way to know what they need is to really listen. Listen to their tone of voice. Sometimes when I meet someone and say, "How are you?" they respond with, "Oh, I'm fine." I detect something in their tone and say, "You don't sound very confident with that answer." Because I listened, this often leads to deeper sharing.

Look at what their eyes reveal. There are times when we'll see fear, anxiety, or tears. Observe body language. Signs such as quivering hands or biting the lip show that the person is crying out. At these times, it's appropriate to say, "How can I help?" A listening presence is remembered much more than a lengthy speech. Be a friend.

SIMPLE TO DO ▸ Most of us know someone who's been crushed by life. They need to be heard. Go to them. Listen with your ears and your eyes. Allow them to get everything out. A shared hurt is easier to bear.

FOLLOW IT THROUGH ▸ *Jesus, my friend, help me always be sensitive to the other person's needs and really listen. Amen.*

MARCH 30 ■ Wednesday of the Fourth Week

ISAIAH 49:8–15 • JOHN 5:17–30

Love Now, Here's How!

"He not only broke the Sabbath, but he also called God his own father." » JOHN 5:18

When I ask people if they feel happy and fulfilled in their relationships, the most common responses I receive are: "I guess so," "Some of the time," and "I haven't thought much about it."

My life, like yours, has been a long series of interwoven relationships. These relationships have been living lessons that have taught me the value of meeting defeat, letting go, and overcoming fear. They have helped me become more open, curious, eager to learn, and accepting of change. A loving relationship should be real. We should love without a mask or hidden agenda. Many of us are much better at claiming to love than we are at actually loving.

For example, we promise to pray for someone, and then we don't. We smile when a person is talking but really don't listen. We tell an acquaintance to call anytime, but when we see their number on our caller ID, we don't pick up the phone. We say, "We'll keep in touch" when we know we won't.

SIMPLE TO DO ▸ Put sincerity into action. In other words, do what is right even when you don't want to. Do the loving thing first and you will enrich your life by building genuine and loving relationships.

FOLLOW IT THROUGH ▸ *Jesus, my friend, help me learn to love. Guide me to recognize opportunities where I can express appreciation and care for others. Amen.*

MARCH 31 ▪ Thursday of the Fourth Week

EXODUS 32:7–14 • JOHN 5:31–47

Choose Gratitude

"He was a burning and shining lamp."
» JOHN 5:35

We grumble about all kinds of things. We complain about the weather, high prices, and even the way God runs the universe.

Some people seem to grumble all the time. They have the marvelous ability to suck the life out of any party. Nothing is ever good enough. They never recognize the sweet satisfaction of contentment. Like a virus, they infect those around them. After talking to them we feel depleted and exhausted.

A grumbler is a person who resists the gifts that God has given. God wants us to receive all these gifts with trust and joy.

We can tone down the grumbling and turn up the gratitude by living a positive, calm, and trusting life. We can let go of resentment, avoid conflict, and refuse to engage in slander or backbiting behavior. When we do, we can shine like a lighthouse and be a soothing voice and presence for others.

SIMPLE TO DO ▸ We all grumble at some time or another. The key is to be conscious of it. Ask your spouse or a friend to alert you if you start making grumbling sounds. This reminder can encourage you to become a beam of light by changing your behavior and feeling gratitude for everything in your life.

FOLLOW IT THROUGH ▸ *Jesus, my friend, help me become more conscious of the good things in my life and choose an attitude of gratitude. Amen.*

APRIL 1 ▪ Friday of the Fourth Week

WISDOM 2:1A, 12–22 • JOHN 7:1–2, 10, 25–30

Friends for Life

"I know him, because I am from him, and he sent me."
» JOHN 7:29

To go through life without a true friend is to have missed one of the most satisfying of human experiences. Many of us take our friendships for granted. We forget that they need constant effort, care, and attention. We share our personal thoughts, feelings, ideas, plans, and dreams with our friends. Friends help us see our imperfections. They give us permission to make mistakes. They give us the strength to meet frustration and even failure.

A while ago, a very special friend of mine died. For over twenty years, we valued and nurtured our friendship. We were often separated, but we made a vow never to allow anything to interfere with our growing friendship. I think often of my friend, our different experiences, the changes we both went through, and the bond that made us friends for life.

Losing a friend is very painful, but having had a true friend means I now have so much more to offer to my present relationships and those to come.

SIMPLE TO DO ▶ Call your friend today. Go to lunch. Spend quality time with each other. Let your friend know what he or she means to you. Share your feelings with a small gift of thanks that your friend will appreciate and understand.

FOLLOW IT THROUGH ▶ *Jesus, you know all about me, and yet you love me anyway. Thank you for being my very special friend. Amen.*

APRIL 2 ▪ Saturday of the Fourth Week ▪ *Saint Francis of Paola*

JEREMIAH 11:18–20 • JOHN 7:40–53

Rethink Your Priorities

"Does our law condemn a person before it first hears him and finds out what he is doing?" » JOHN 7:51

A friend invited me to his magic show. Just before the performance, a woman approached my table and asked if she could sit next to me. I nodded, and we shook hands and exchanged names. After a few minutes, she said, "I've got to tell you that I'm really shaken up inside. I just received a call that a dear friend died.

"You know," she went on, "something like this causes one to think of how important it is to live in the moment. You never really know what's going to happen." And in that moment, this woman was rethinking her priorities: all the things in her life that really mattered most.

Priorities are important, and we all have them. But life is always in motion and constantly changing. A hundred years from now, it will not matter what our bank balance was. What will matter is what we chose to give our time and energy to. What will it be for you?

SIMPLE TO DO ▶ List the top five priorities of your life. Can you accomplish any of these today? This week? This Lent? Set a goal for meeting your priorities and stick to it.

FOLLOW IT THROUGH ▶ *Jesus, my friend, I don't want to spend all my energy and time on the small stuff. Help me recognize and make room for the things that really are important. Amen.*

APRIL 3 ▪ Fifth Sunday of Lent

ISAIAH 43:16–21 • PHILIPPIANS 3:8–14 • JOHN 8:1–11 *or*,
FOR YEAR A: EZEKIEL 37:12–14 • ROMANS 8:8–11 • JOHN 11:1–45 *or* 11:3–7, 17, 20–27, 33B–45

Look in the Mirror First

"If anyone of you is without sin, be the first to throw a stone."
» JOHN 8:7

Oh, to have a heart that doesn't judge! It's so easy to project our thoughts and feelings onto someone else. We don't know another person's struggles or motives. We don't know their situation. Most of all, we don't know their hearts. When we judge, we build walls between others and ourselves. We put too much weight on a first impression. How many potentially good friends have we lost simply because we judged them on our first impression?

Maybe we ourselves are living with someone's judgment. They may have formed a negative opinion based on difficulties we've had in the past with legal problems, financial struggles, substance abuse, divorce, or emotional issues. Jesus did not join the rock throwers who found fault with the woman accused of adultery. Instead, he invited her into a caring relationship by taking the time to enter her world, calm her fear, and challenge her to change.

When we judge others and jump to negative conclusions, we create resistance in our relationships. We need instead to understand their personality, gifts, wounds, struggles, and joys.

SIMPLE TO DO ▷ Is there someone you have prejudged? If so, apologize. Applaud them for improvements made and positive steps taken.

FOLLOW IT THROUGH ▷ *Jesus, my friend, I want to see people with your eyes, hushing any judgments that pop into my head. Amen.*

APRIL 4 ▪ Monday of the Fifth Week ▪ *Saint Isidore*

DANIEL 13:1–9, 15–17, 19–30, 33–62 *or* 13:41C–62 • JOHN 8:12–20

Possibilities Are Everywhere

"Whoever follows me will not walk in darkness."
» JOHN 8:12

There are times in life when everything seems hopeless. Each of us can relate to the suffocating feeling of being overwhelmed, outnumbered, or surrounded—where the odds were stacked against us.

You may find yourself in a crisis right now through no fault of your own, created by circumstances beyond your control. Whatever it is, you see no way out. But don't give up. You do have choices! You can allow what has happened, or what may or may not happen, to fill your head with negative, hopeless thinking—or you can hope.

Never give up, ever; there is always hope, a feeling of optimism that good things will come. Looking back on our lives, we can see that we did make it through the hassles and circumstances we feared the most. Hope means that we believe deep down inside that good things will happen. It gives us the motivation to go on day after day and to be hope-bearers for others, encouraging them to hang on, no matter what.

SIMPLE TO DO ▶ Make a creative Hope Basket for those going through difficult times. Fill it with flowers, positive quotes, prayers, poems, Bible verses, or cartoons. Give it to someone who really needs it and encourage them to never give up.

FOLLOW IT THROUGH ▶ *Jesus, my friend, when I feel I cannot take one more step, you are behind me giving me a big push. Thank you so much. Amen.*

APRIL 5 ■ Tuesday of the Fifth Week ■ *Saint Vincent Ferrer*

NUMBERS 21:4–9 • JOHN 8:21–30

Wishing upon Your Own Star

"You will surely die in your sins unless you come to believe."
» JOHN 8:24

For every up in life, there is a down; for every triumph, there is a challenge. But our resiliency is determined by our ability to like ourselves. Liking ourselves is as essential as breathing. Without it, we make bad decisions, push our loved ones away, and prevent ourselves from achieving our goals.

Many people dislike themselves. They often feel they have no value and nothing to offer. They are not aware of their intrinsic value and God-given worth.

We have to be willing to draw our value from what God has given us. We are uniquely fashioned: an exclusive combination that will never happen again. We have to be willing to stand up proudly and say: "I am special. I am one of a kind. I am terrific. I am learning. I am growing. I am changing. I am God's child. I am a masterpiece created by the Master Artist."

Relax and enjoy who you are. Remember, you don't have to rehearse to be yourself, and it can be a lot of fun.

SIMPLE TO DO ▶ Write the following words on colorful post-it notes: "I like myself just the way I am," or "I am somebody," and paste these on the mirrors and doors in your house.

FOLLOW IT THROUGH ▶ *Jesus, my friend, I will stop comparing myself to others. No one can do a better job of being me than me. Amen.*

APRIL 6 ■ Wednesday of the Fifth Week
DANIEL 3:14–20, 91–92, 95 • JOHN 8:31–42

The Truth, the Whole Truth

"You will know the truth, and the truth will set you free."
» JOHN 8:32

Jesus put a great deal of emphasis on speaking the truth, and it is the basic foundation of all our relationships.

If we're consistent in telling the truth about the small stuff, it will build character and cause us to honor the truth about the really big stuff. So tell the truth about how much weight you actually lost or how much time you really spent on a project. Do not exaggerate. Instead of saying, "I can't do this," be honest and say, "You know, I'm really not interested in doing this." People will be surprised, and they will appreciate your frankness. Sometimes, dishonesty covers up the problem and the solution to the problem. Lying or trying to hide the truth is offensive and may cause us to drift into an uncomfortable connection because of mistrust or suspicion.

Speaking the truth will always improve our relationships. Being truthful is simply revealing the facts. The more facts we have, the more we'll understand, and the more likely we'll come up with the answers we're looking for.

SIMPLE TO DO ▶ If dishonesty has claimed some of the love you could be having in your relationship, how do you plan to resolve the situation? Sit down and create a strategy and be open to what you might hear.

FOLLOW IT THROUGH ▶ *Jesus, my friend, the truth that has made me free will also make me happy. Amen.*

APRIL 7 ■ Thursday of the Fifth Week ■ *Saint John Baptist de la Salle*

GENESIS 17:3–9 • JOHN 8:51–59

Live Like There's No Tomorrow

"Amen, I say to you, whoever keeps my word will never see death." » JOHN 8:51

At sixteen, Sam was diagnosed with stomach cancer. The doctors tried every treatment available, but after eighteen months, nothing more could be done. Sam was not afraid. His serenity came from a decision he made only months before the initial diagnosis. He said, "I'm going to live until I die." With that decision, Sam made his peace with death.

We often see death as terrible and tragic. Because we want so much to live, we view death as the enemy. The more we deny it, the more monstrous it becomes.

But death is a friend that brings our existence into focus. The mere thought of it helps us sort out our priorities so we can live a meaningful life. It nudges us to take care of the most important things first.

Life can be difficult. It can bruise us and bang us around, but how we respond to it determines its quality. Death is not the final word. Life is. Jesus slammed the door on death and rendered it powerless.

SIMPLE TO DO ▶ Focus on your blessings rather than your struggles. Smell the roses. Spend time in nature. Whistle while you work. Practice gratitude. Share quality moments with the people you love.

FOLLOW IT THROUGH ▶ *Jesus, my friend, help me welcome death as a friend. Remind me to live, love, laugh, and learn—now. Amen.*

APRIL 8 ▪ Friday of the Fifth Week

JEREMIAH 20:10–13 • JOHN 10:31–42

What to Do with Critics

"We are not stoning you for a good work but for blasphemy. You are making yourself God." » JOHN 10:33

During my early years in ministry, I was so insecure that I immediately became defensive and angry whenever I was criticized. Now when I'm confronted or judged, the first thing I do is ask myself: "Is there any truth in it?"

Perhaps criticism shows up in our lives to help us change and grow. So how should we respond to it? Some of us avoid making a clear and direct response. Any disapproval is perceived as a threat. Because of this, we feel the need to defend ourselves. We reject the critic and turn the conversation into an attack on their character.

It's possible, however, to embrace criticism as an opportunity to grow. We don't get mad, make excuses, or retaliate. We consider the value of the criticism and make a decision to implement any necessary changes.

SIMPLE TO DO ▸ Before you start to criticize another person, ask yourself: Do I have all the information? Is my criticism necessary, relevant, and meaningful? Am I seeking to help the person or destroy them? If you ask these questions beforehand and answer them honestly, you will spend less time repairing any damage or retracting your words later.

FOLLOW IT THROUGH ▸ *Jesus, my friend, I know I cannot please everyone. I make plenty of mistakes. Allow me to be open to the comments of those who care about me so I can change and grow. Amen.*

APRIL 9 ■ Saturday of the Fifth Week
EZEKIEL 37:21–28 • JOHN 11:45–56

Count Your Blessings

"What are we going to do? This man is performing many signs and people are believing in him." » JOHN 11:47–48

When Diane wistfully talked about her friend's new house, she found herself grumbling, wishing her own home were bigger and better.

Envy! Most often, we envy our friends. Why did their son get the solo in the school concert and mine didn't? Why did he get a promotion and I didn't? How does she manage to look so together and I don't? Envy can easily turn companions into competitors. Instead of promoting closeness and unity, envy leads to animosity, distance, and malicious slander. Our agenda becomes anything that will tear the other person down and build us up.

There's a remedy for envy: get up every single day and count your blessings by focusing on the gifts you have been given. We can curb envy by cherishing the talents we have, the people in our lives, and the opportunities before us. If your primary problem is envy, pay attention to the wisdom of Claudian, a fourth-century Latin poet: "Those who envy are always poor."

SIMPLE TO DO ▶ Every day, for one week, write down ten new blessings you are grateful for. Thank God for them and celebrate them.

FOLLOW IT THROUGH ▶ *Jesus, my friend, a funny thing happens when I count my blessings: the more I count, the more they show up. Thank you. Amen.*

APRIL 10 ■ Palm Sunday of the Passion of the Lord

LUKE 19:28–40 • ISAIAH 50:4–7 • PHILIPPIANS 2:6–11 • LUKE 22:14—23:56 or 23:1–49

"Oops!" Moments

"We are receiving what we deserve for our deeds; but this man has done nothing wrong." » LUKE 23:41

Presiding at my first wedding as a priest, I wanted everything to be perfect. Things went flawlessly at the rehearsal. But the next day, just as the wedding started, the air conditioner kicked on from the vent above me. The air caught my notes and carried them up over the wedding party. They hung motionless for one dramatic second, and then dove down and slid under the second row of pews. Oops!

Our lives are filled with such moments. Often, we try to blame our mistakes and embarrassments on someone else. We blame our parents, our genes, our teacher, our spouse. But when we blame others, we give up the power to change.

Accepting the blame takes only a few magical words: "I'm sorry. I made a mistake. Please forgive me." Acknowledging our oops! moments keeps us "real." In church that day, when my papers went soaring, I cracked a joke that broke the tension. Make light of your "Oops!" and it lodges forever as a happy memory.

SIMPLE TO DO ▶ Practice saying these words: "I'm sorry. I made a mistake. Please forgive me." Feel how good it is to concentrate on loving and not blaming.

FOLLOW IT THROUGH ▶ *Jesus, my friend, once I take my life into my own hands, a remarkable thing happens: I feel powerful because no one is left to blame. Amen.*

APRIL 11 ■ Monday of Holy Week

ISAIAH 42:1–7 • JOHN 12:1–11

Choose Your Friends Carefully

He said this not because he cared for the poor, but because he was a thief and used to steal the contributions. » JOHN 12:6

Our friends are those who have seen us at our worst and still love us. They have survived our anger, dried our tears, and sat with us in hospital waiting rooms. We could spend a good portion of our lives looking out for ourselves. Judas did. Mary didn't. Judas grabbed from life; Mary gave to it.

The grabbers sap our energy and our strength. They want to be with us as long as we bring them value. They talk at us, not to us. They don't listen. They monopolize a conversation so the focus will stay on them. The givers, however, call and say, "I'm thinking of you. I care." When we do need them, they show up early and often, without an agenda.

It seems like an odd prescription for happiness, but some of the most joyful times in our lives are when we freely give of ourselves to a person in need without expecting anything in return. In those times, we feel a deep joy unlike anything else.

SIMPLE TO DO ▸ Work on being a giver. Help someone clean up without being asked, volunteer to visit, or do something that will please someone. Be a true friend!

FOLLOW IT THROUGH ▸ *Jesus, my friend, during your entire life you made the needs of others more important than your own. Help me follow your example. Amen.*

APRIL 12 ■ Tuesday of Holy Week

ISAIAH 49:1-6 • JOHN 13:21-33, 36-38

Watch Your Back

"Amen, amen, I say to you, one of you will betray me."
» JOHN 13:21

Betrayal can be so painful. Our closest friends know our darkest secrets. They have the power to hurt us precisely because they know us so well. If this happens, we have a choice: we can slam the door shut and keep it locked with anger, or we can slowly learn to forgive.

It is possible to genuinely forgive someone who has betrayed us. In fact, I've found in my own life that when I've fully forgiven someone, I've gained tremendous insight into myself and others. Compassion has increased my ability to forgive by leaps and bounds.

Remember, when we forgive those who betray us, we are doing it for ourselves, to take care of ourselves. When we refuse to forgive, we continue to hurt ourselves. We are letting the one who betrayed us keep control of our emotions and actions. When we let go and truly forgive, we are free once again.

SIMPLE TO DO ▶ Let your anger out safely. If you need to release it, find a way that doesn't hurt anyone. Some people go jogging, hammer nails, pound a punching bag, or scream. Let it all out and then forgive.

FOLLOW IT THROUGH ▶ *Jesus, my friend, I have experienced a friend's betrayal. If I am still holding on to my anger, help me truly forgive, so my pain and anger will soften and perhaps even disappear over time. Amen.*

APRIL 13 ▪ Wednesday of Holy Week

ISAIAH 50:4–9A • MATTHEW 26:14–25

We're All in This Together

"Surely, it is not I, Rabbi?" » MATTHEW 26:25

Families wrestle with it. Psychologists argue over it. Churches preach about it. Mostly we just feel it—guilt—deep in our soul. Some professional counselors even say that guilt is the cornerstone of all serious problems. If we're ever going to deal with guilt, we need to understand: we're all in this together. All of us have done something wrong. Getting rid of guilt starts with a truthful self-evaluation. Anyone who's been in a twelve-step program knows about Step Four: take a fearless moral inventory. It involves action, faith, and hope.

Here's the action: make a list of all the things you've done that have caused harm to others and yourself. Write each one down as it comes to mind. Making this list is not simple. It takes courage, energy, honesty, and prayer. God will give you the strength you need.

It's time to stop rationalizing, excusing, and blaming others. Come clean. We must own what we have done. We cannot be right with God until we accept responsibility for our actions. Until we recognize that we are wrong, we cannot know the peace that comes from God's forgiveness.

SIMPLE TO DO ▶ Make your list and then practice acknowledgment and alteration to wipe the slate clean.

FOLLOW IT THROUGH ▶ *Jesus, my friend, I want to come clean with what I have done. I want to experience the joy of your forgiving love. Amen.*

APRIL 14 ■ Thursday of Holy Week (Holy Thursday)

CHRISM MASS: ISAIAH 61:1–3A, 6A, 8B–9 • REVELATION 1:5–8 • LUKE 4:16–21
EVENING MASS OF THE LORD'S SUPPER: EXODUS 12:1–8, 11–14 •
1 CORINTHIANS 11:23–26 • JOHN 13:1–15

How Do You Want to Be Remembered?

"Do you realize what I have done to you?" » JOHN 13:12

The disciples were always on the road with Jesus as he was preaching, teaching, healing, and repeatedly being challenged or criticized. On this evening, Jesus had one last chance to say to them, "This is who I really am; this is how I want you to remember me."

Who were they remembering? A teacher who did all he said he would do. With an open heart, he made himself touchable, vulnerable, and approachable. Those bruised by life asked, "Is there anyone who can help me?" Jesus was their answer.

He offered them compassion, love, and acceptance. This was running through the minds of the disciples as they shared their last meal with Jesus: memories of the sick being healed, the weak becoming strong, outcasts being welcomed, the dying knowing peace, and sinners being given a fresh start. Jesus offered relief from pain and healing, and we can do the same.

SIMPLE TO DO ▶ Try to include those who are alone in your Easter celebration. There are elderly people who have no family, parents whose children are far away, couples who are separated due to military service, and those who are alone because of family problems. Be alert to these people and include them in your celebrations.

FOLLOW IT THROUGH ▶ *Jesus, my friend, I want to be remembered for the difference I make in the lives of people who are hurting. Amen.*

APRIL 15 ■ Friday of the Passion of the Lord (Good Friday)

ISAIAH 52:13—53:12 • HEBREWS 4:14-16; 5:7-9 • JOHN 18:1—19:42

I Am Bigger Than You!

"You have no power over me." » JOHN 19:11

Advice columnist Ann Landers was once asked for the most important advice she could offer everyone. She wrote in reply: "Trouble is an inevitable part of your life, and when it comes, hold your head high, look it squarely in the eye, and say, 'I am bigger than you; you cannot defeat me.'"

The more we dwell on our problems, the bigger they become. We begin to react negatively, engage in self-doubt, make poor choices, feel rejected, push God away, get discouraged, and isolate ourselves. So stop dwelling on them! Let your challenges be your teachers. Believe that troubles can turn into triumphs. Choose to adapt, adjust, and advance. Focus on opportunities, not liabilities. Then let go and move on. This makes us stronger, wiser, healthier, and more compassionate.

Jesus knew what awaited him. Even though his closest disciples had abandoned him, he rose above their rejection and took up his cross. He knew who he was. God is in our lives. The Shepherd is taking care of his sheep. Because of this we too can look trouble squarely in the eye and, like Jesus at the moment of his death, we can say, *I am bigger than you; you cannot defeat me.*

SIMPLE TO DO ▶ Spend some time today in silent prayer. Reflect on an area of difficulty in your life, knowing that Jesus, who died for us, is there with you.

FOLLOW IT THROUGH ▶ *Jesus, my friend, I am grateful for my problems. They have helped me grow in ways I could never have imagined. Amen.*

APRIL 16 ■ Holy Saturday (Easter Vigil)

GENESIS 1:1—2:2 or 1:1, 26–31A ● GENESIS 22:1–18 or 22:1–2, 9A, 10–13, 15–18 ● EXODUS 14:15—15:1 ● ISAIAH 54:5–14 ● ISAIAH 55:1–11 ● BARUCH 3:9–15, 32—4:4 ● EZEKIEL 36:16–17A, 18–28 ● ROMANS 6:3–11 ● LUKE 24:1–12

Never Give Up!

"He is not here...he has been raised." » LUKE 24:6

Many of us have trouble focusing on the good stuff because of devastating past experiences. What do we do when our world collapses? After the dust has cleared we can learn something about ourselves. Only then do we discover our deepest resources and our spiritual strength. Whether it's a broken heart, a faded dream, or just something that hasn't gone right, consider the following three lessons.

1. Look (don't linger) at the problem. Use positive thoughts to discover the hidden lessons you need.
2. Latch onto (don't lose) a determined attitude. Ask yourself: Does this setback deserve the reaction I'm giving it? Usually, it does not.
3. Let (don't limit) God, who can use discouragement for our good. Though the darkness is real, it is not greater than God's ability to see us through to the other side.

As disciples of Jesus, we believe that darkness will never overcome the light. This is the promise of Easter.

SIMPLE TO DO ▶ Make an encouragement basket filled with a dozen plastic Easter eggs. Fill the eggs with uplifting quotes or personal notes and give the basket to someone who feels like giving up.

FOLLOW IT THROUGH ▶ *Jesus, my friend, just when I wonder if I can take any more, you push me and keep me moving. Thank you! Amen.*

ALSO BY JOSEPH SICA

Fr. Joe Sica believes that no matter how deep our sorrows, how big our mistakes, or how firmly we hold on to our grudges, Jesus always stands ready to help us free ourselves so that we can live in love, forgiveness, and joy. Filled with humor, prayer, real-life stories, and very practical steps, *Your Guide to a Happy Life* brings together some of Fr. Joe's most powerful reflections to help you reach for the loving, joyous life Jesus wants you to have.

80 PAGES | $12.95 | 5½" x 8½" | 9781627855648

TO ORDER CALL 1-800-321-0411
OR VISIT WWW.TWENTYTHIRDPUBLICATIONS.COM

TWENTY-THIRD PUBLICATIONS
A division of Bayard, Inc.